The Church of God as Revealed in Scripture

by
Arlo F. Newell
Author of Receive the Holy Spirit

Published by
Warner Press, Inc.
Anderson, Indiana

i

Copyright © by Warner Press, Inc.
ISBN 0-87162-269-6
All Rights Reserved
Printed in the United States of America
Warner Press, Inc.
Arlo F. Newell, Editor in Chief

To my wife, Helen, a growing person, dear friend, inquisitive scholar, and constant companion in our quest for truth

Contents

Introduction

The Church of God revealed in Scripture stands distinct from the denominational concepts of this present world. Rather than a church of systems, institutions, and dogmatic discipline, it is revealed as God's truth that produced a people peculiarly (1 Pet. 2:9) his own. Through preaching (*kerygma*) and teaching (*didache*) of this revealed truth, God raised up a people called out (*ecclesia*) from the world to be the body of Christ, the Church.

It is the intent of this small volume to acquaint the reader with the religious beliefs that helped to shape and mold the Church of God. Purchased and established by Christ (Acts 20:28), the Church was inaugurated on the Day of Pentecost as the Holy Ghost filled the 120 believers gathered in the Upper Room (Acts 2:4). From this representative community God gave the pattern for this faithful remnant—a pattern presented in Scripture as the Holy Spirit inspired (2 Pet. 1:71) the writing of that Word that endures forever (1 Pet. 1:25).

1

While the Word stands sure across the ages, our treatment and interpretation of that Word has not always been reliable or trustworthy. We are affected by the cultural winds of evangelicalism, fundamentalism, and/or liberalism. History reveals that the Church was confronted by infidelity from without and heresies from within. While outward persecution served to establish the young Church more firmly, heresy within created an apostasy that produced the Dark Ages. Apostasy literally means "desertion of the faith." Because of periods of severe persecution it became expedient for some to desert the faith once delivered unto the saints. Rather than Holy Spirit rule, it became easier for human authority, ritualism, forms, and creeds to control the religious community, thus quenching the truth that sets us free.

In the midst of such critical conditions, however, God preserved a sacred remnant who remained faithful in their quest for and obedience to the truth. Thus, from the darkness there emerged the reforms that called God's people back to biblical truth. Martin Luther in Germany and the Wesleys in England became representatives of reformers who dared to stand for truth in its finest theological and practical interpretation. The faithfulness of such persons past and present serves as a spiritual catalyst, causing us to reflect upon the pattern of the Church of God revealed in Scripture.

Out of such a quest for scriptural truth God moved in the year 1880 upon the heart of Daniel Sidney Warner and others, calling Christendom to holiness and oneness. Being led by the Holy Spirit

2

into an understanding of scriptural holiness, D. S. Warner saw this as the key to Christian unity. He believed that the experience of holiness must eventuate in the unity of God's people. It was a unity in Christ that went beyond sectarian spirits and denominational doctrine. Therefore, he declared himself free from all humanly instituted religion and began to fellowship all persons who had experienced the lordship of Christ.

Out of the moving of the Spirit among persons of all faiths, other Christians in many parts of the nation were being led into a similar understanding of true unity. With a spirit of humility they sought only to follow Christ rather than humanly organized religious orders of their day. Being committed to this truth and drawn together by the Holy Spirit as a voluntary fellowship of believers, this movement has continued to grow over the past century. Recognizing only the lordship of Christ, they have sincerely sought God's plan for the Church. They have avoided creedalism and doctrinal disciplines, seeking only to have the Bible as their rule of faith. While acknowledging that this allows for diversity within the fellowship, it also makes possible a unity that is divinely originated rather than humanly instituted. The beauty of God's Church is the unity that comes from a common experience of holiness, producing lives obedient to Christ, the head of the Church.

To help acquaint you with the Bible, we have endeavored to accentuate those doctrines most evident in the Church of God as revealed in Scripture. Such theological truth is vital to the life of each Christian and to every church. What we

3

believe as doctrine does make a difference. While some religious bodies may periodically revise their theological positions, there are truths in Scripture that are forever settled and that the Holy Spirit reveals to those who seek to know God's will.

As a movement of God's people we desire to know those truths and to make them known to others. Having committed ourselves to truth, we must pursue it all the days of our lives rather than yield to the temptation of tradition. It is our prayer that this brief introduction compiled from writings of Church of God authors will help you to understand God's Word as the Holy Spirit reveals to you the Church and her teachings.

In no way is this to be interpreted as a definitive statement of the doctrines of the Church of God. We are not a denomination. It is not intended to satisfy the theologian or placate the absolutist. However, we do hope that it will give helpful guidance to basic Christian beliefs, thus enabling the student of the Bible to experience a living theology that is applicable to a meaningful Christian life in this present hour as we are led to unity by the Spirit of Truth.

Arlo F. Newell
Editor in Chief
Warner Press, Inc.
Anderson, Indiana

June, 1983

Chapter 1

God: His Self-Revelation

"**I**n the beginning God" opens to us the sacred Scriptures and focuses attention upon our Creator and Lord. Such a beginning leaves no room for debate; the inspired writers accept the existence of God. However, within each person is a rational intuitiveness that desires to know God more completely. "Bare belief in a higher power is intuitive — is simply one of those innate truths, fundamental facts, or drives, or urges. This intuitive idea is not the conclusion but the beginning of the process."[1]

Regardless of one's religious or nonreligious background, there is a quest to know God. In response to this quest and God's grace, the Lord has chosen to reveal himself to us in the Bible. Here alone in Scripture do we find God adequately revealed in acts of creation and through his Son,

Jesus Christ. While not being able to fully comprehend all of God's nature, we do see in Scripture these attributes that enable us to know our Maker:

1. *Self-existence.* "The Father has life in himself" (John 5:26). "For with thee is the fountain of life" (Ps. 36:9). He is underived and inexhaustible.

2. *Eternity.* "Before the mountains were brought forth, or ever thou hadst formed the earth and the world, from everlasting to everlasting thou art God" (Ps. 90:2). "The high and lofty One who inhabits eternity" (Isa. 57:15).

3. *Spirituality.* "God is Spirit" (John 4:24).

4. *Unity.* There is one true and living God. "There is no other god besides me" (Isa. 45:21).

5. *Immutability.* "I the Lord do not change" (Mal. 3:6). "The Father of lights, with whom there is no variation, neither shadow of turning" (James 1:17).

6. *Omnipresence.* He is everywhere present. "Can a man hide himself in secret places so that I cannot see him? says the Lord. Do I not fill heaven and earth?" (Jer. 23:24). He is "not far from each one of us, for 'In him we live and move and have our being' " (Acts 17:27–28).

7. *Omniscience.* He is all-knowing. "Who has made these things known from of old" (Acts 15:18). "And before him no creature is hidden, but all are open and laid bare to the eyes of him with whom we have to do" (Heb. 4:13).

8. *Omnipotence.* He has unlimited and universal power. "His eternal power and deity" (Rom. 1:20). "With God all things are possible" (Matt. 19:26).

9. *Wisdom.* "Blessed be the name of God forever and ever, to whom belong wisdom and might" (Dan. 2:20). "O the depth of the riches and wisdom and knowledge of God! How unsearchable are his judgments, and how inscrutable his ways!" (Rom. 11:33).

10. *Holiness and truth.* "I am holy" (1 Pet. 1:16). "Thou who art of purer eyes than to behold evil, and canst not look on wrong" (Hab. 1:13). "God, who never lies" (Titus 1:2).

11. *Justice.* God demands righteousness of all his intelligent creatures, and he deals righteously with them. "Righteousness and justice are the foundation of thy throne" (Ps. 89:14). "But in every nation any one who fears him, and does what is right is acceptable to him" (Acts 10:35).

12. *Goodness.* He is benevolent, loving, merciful, and gracious. "The riches of his kindness" (Rom. 2:4). "God so loved the world" (John 3:16). "His steadfast love endures forever" (Ps. 136). "The God of all grace" (1 Pet. 5:10).

13. *Faithfulness.* "The Lord is faithful" (2 Thess. 3:3). "Sarah . . . considered him faithful who had promised" (Heb. 11:11).[2]

However, the grace of God chose to reveal this divine love. Grace emphasizes the fact that God is for us, even when we are against him and ourselves. This concern for us is not determined by our response, but by God's redemptive love as expressed in Christ. Knowing what was in humanity, God demonstrated divine grace as he revealed himself in Jesus Christ and as he died for the world's redemption. This amazing grace of God brought to us the living Word and revealed his

7

unlimited love. "In the beginning was the Word, and the Word was with God, and the Word was God. . . . And the Word became flesh and dwelt among us, full of grace and truth" (John 1:1,14). "For God so loved the world that he gave his only Son, that whoever believes in him should not perish but have eternal life" (John 3:16).

Having exemplified such grace through the expression of the living Word, one recognizes that it is the grace of God that makes possible our salvation and continued growth in Christ.

"For by grace you have been saved through faith; and this is not your own doing, it is the gift of God — not because of works, lest any man should boast" (Eph. 2:8 – 9).

"For the grace of God has appeared for the salvation of all men, training us to renounce irreligion and worldly passions, and to live sober, upright, and godly lives in this world" (Titus 2:11 – 12). "But grow in the grace and knowledge of our Lord and Savior Jesus Christ" (2 Pet. 3:18).

God was not obligated to redeem us, but out of the graciousness of his very being he chose to reveal himself through the Bible as the Word instructs us in true righteousness. Humanity, therefore, is without excuse if we fail to respond to this grace extended. It is freely given to all, to be joyfully and humbly accepted as we believe in God as revealed through Scripture.

The Inspired Word

Properly understood, the Bible should be called the Word of God. Containing sixty-six books, thirty-nine in the Old Testament and twenty-seven in the New Testament, it comprises for all the world God's revelation of himself and his people, the Church. Transmitted first by oral tradition, it was then written on papyrus scrolls, with manuscripts being preserved across the centuries. While not possessing any of the original manuscripts or first editions, the people of God have preserved sufficient documents to communicate to us the Christian faith.

Without question, the Bible is of divine origin, produced by persons from all walks of life as they were inspired by the Holy Spirit; therefore, it is rightly referred to as the Word of God. Both the Old and New Testaments are recognized for their divine inspiration. The term *scriptures* as used in 2 Timothy 3:16 refers to the Old Testament writings possessed at the time of Paul. These Old Testament writings pointed toward the coming of Christ, the Messiah, the living embodiment of the Word. In this context the *inspired* Word, though recorded by persons like ourselves, becomes the expression of God's will. "Inspiration is that influence of the Spirit of God upon the minds of the Scripture writers which made their writings the record of a progressive divine revelation, sufficient when taken together and interpreted by the same Spirit who inspired them, to lead every honest inquirer to Christ and salvation."[3]

One cannot help but be amazed at the Word of God; it is simple and yet reliable, fully trustworthy, and authoritative. Isaiah wrote, "Fools shall not err therein" (35:8). While containing profound truths about all of life, it is so simple that the most unlearned person may recognize and experience God's grace.

The Word of God is forever settled; therefore, it is absolute in its authority and final in its judgments. More than mere human thought, the Word of God is the result of God and humanity working together. Peter wrote, "Men moved by the Holy Spirit spoke from God" (2 Pet. 1:21). God gave to these inspired writers an understanding of the sin of the human race and of God's solution to our sin. In dealing with the source of our predicament, Scripture helps us to see beyond where we are to where we can be by God's grace. God is still revealing himself to us today. And while we may have come to an understanding of some truth, we must continue to be receptive to new truth as the Holy Spirit leads us into a deeper knowledge of God's grace.

Questions for Study, Chapter 1

1. How did God choose to reveal himself?
   Titus 2:11 _____

   _____

2. In what manner did the inspired writers explain their belief in the existence of God as Creator?
   Genesis 1:1 _____

   Exodus 3:14 _____

3. List seven of the attributes of God given in this chapter.
   1._____
   2._____
   3._____
   4._____
   5._____
   6._____
   7._____

4. Define *grace* in your own words. (See Ephesians 2:8–9; 2 Peter 3:18.)

   _____

   _____

11

5. To what was Paul referring when he spoke of "scriptures" in 2 Timothy 3:16?

_____

_____

6. Explain the term inspiration as understood in this chapter.

_____

_____

_____

7. How many books are in the Old Testament?_____

The New Testament? _____

Now please name all the books of the Bible as you share them with a friend.

Memorize:

Before the mountains were brought forth or ever thou hadst formed the earth and the world, from everlasting to everlasting thou art God.

— Psalm 90:2

Chapter 2

Sin: The Human Problem

As Creator, God made us in his own image (Gen. 1:27). He gave of himself that we might be moral beings who exercise the freedom of the will and use the intelligence entrusted to us as spiritual beings. In this original state humanity was like God, living in holiness and purity, exercising the power of choice in determining personal conduct.

Being so richly endowed, people possessed the possibility of choosing to do right or wrong. God wanted his creation to respond in loving obedience rather than because of legal order. When confronted by a choice between good and evil, sin entered into God's moral universe. Exercising free moral choice, our foreparents willfully chose to disobey God's command (Gen. 3:1–7), and thus came the consequent suffering of universal sinfulness. The Pauline writings emphasize for us the

13

fact of universal sin because of this disobedience. "For as in Adam all die, so also in Christ shall all be made alive" (1 Cor. 15:22).

Paul knew that only as people recognize their sinfulness will they be able to fully understand the plan of salvation revealed in God's Word. Therefore, it was necessary that both Jews and Greeks (Rom. 3:9), as well as all others, be made aware of their sinfulness. "There is no distinction; since all have sinned and fall short of the glory of God" (Rom. 3:22–23). Sin in its primary sense is lack of conformity to law. It is the opposite of holiness. The term *sin* is used in two senses: (1) of conduct and (2) of character. In the first, which is the primary use, it is commonly expressed in the New Testament by the Greek term *anomia*, which means contrary to law or without law. Sin in this sense has to do only with conduct, not in the narrow sense of mere human action, but in the broader sense as including thoughts, motives, and volitions. In this sense it is often called actual transgression to distinguish it from sinfulness of character, which is frequently termed original sin or natural depravity. In this latter or secondary sense it has to do with what one *is* rather than with what one *does*. Another Greek term, *harmartia*, is ordinarily used in the New Testament to describe this unholiness of character. Examples of the use of this Greek word are as follows: "When the commandment came, sin revived and I died" (Rom. 7:9). "So then it is no longer I that do it, but sin which dwells within me" (v. 17). Here sin, *hamartia*, is evidently used to designate a derangement or depravity of the nature. In one place, 1

14

John 3:4, *hamartia*, sin, is used as a synonym of *anomia* and is said to be *anomia*, or a transgression of the law.

Sin in conduct may be by commission — doing what should not be done; or by omission — failing to do what should be done. Two standards may be distinguished for judging as to what is sinful: (1) sin in the abstract or absolute sense, and (2) sin in the concrete or imputed sense. In the first view acts are judged in relation to principles of right apart from the actor's knowledge or motives in performing them. For example, according to this view, to speak falsely is regarded as sin even though the speaker is ignorant of the fact that he or she speaks falsely and intends to speak only the truth.

According to the second view, which is the sense in which sin is commonly used of conduct in the New Testament, only those acts are sinful that are prompted by wrong motives. In this view sin is imputed as guilt to one only according to knowledge or intentions. That which is right in itself is imputed as sin to one who esteems it to be evil when he or she performs it. Such is the teaching of the Apostle Paul in regard to the eating of meats and the observing of days. "It is unclean for anyone who thinks it unclean" (Rom. 14:14). Likewise, if for lack of knowledge one does with a good motive that which is in itself a violation of principles of right, it is not imputed to that person as sin, because of the good motive in doing it. In this sense sin is a violation of the greatest commandment on which all others hang. Imputed sin in conduct, then, is a rebellious attitude of heart toward God.

Therefore, sin is imputed to its perpetrator as such only when that person feels a sense of moral obligation and voluntarily chooses that which he or she believes to be wrong. It is not required that the person shall have performed an outward sinful act or spoken an evil word. He or she may sin in thought. "Every one who looks at a woman lustfully has already committed adultery with her in his heart" (Matt. 5:28). Sin is committed in the volition to do what is esteemed to be wrong. Temptation is not sin. When Eve considered the words of the serpent and felt the desire for the forbidden fruit, she had not yet committed sin. She incurred no guilt until of her own free will she decided to do what God had forbidden. God was responsible for the primitive probation. Satan tempted Eve. But neither the fact of probation nor the temptation were determinative of the woman's conduct. She determined that herself. Therefore, God is not the author of sin (James 1:13), but humanity is wholly responsible for it.[4]

The Bible reveals that sin alienates one from God. It is referred to as death, spiritual and physical. New Testament writers compare it to darkness in which there is no light at all. The person in sin is like a sheep lost without a shepherd.

Questions for Study, Chapter 2

1. What do we mean when we speak of the "fall" of Adam and Eve? Genesis 3:1 – 7 _____

_____

2. The universal nature of sin is explained in 1 Corinthians 15:22; please write this in your own words.

_____

3. Are only the Jewish people guilty of rejecting Christ? (See Romans 3:9, 23.) _____

_____

4. The term *sin* is used in two senses: A_____ B_____ What are the Greek terms applied to these: A_____ B_____

5. How does one determine the sinfulness of a deed? (See Romans 14.) Please list the principles in this chapter. _____

_____

_____

6. Is it a sin for one to be tempted? James 1:12 – 14 _____

_____

_____

7. Jesus did not destroy the law but amplified its meaning, acknowledging that it is possible to sin by thought as well as deed. Discover this reference in the Sermon on the Mount. (See Matthew 5.)_____

_____

_____

Memorize:

For all have sinned and come short of the glory of God.

—Romans 3:23

For the wages of sin is death.

—Romans 6:23

Chapter 3

Salvation: God's Plan

Because of our alienation from God our only hope is in the atonement of Christ. Symbolized in the Old Testament through the sacrificial offerings for sin, the atonement found fulfillment in the New Testament. While the atonement is rooted in the nature of God, it was his grace that made provision for our complete redemption through the death of Christ.

"In him we have redemption through his blood, the forgiveness of our trespasses" (Eph. 1:7). "The Son of man came . . . to give his life as a ransom for many" (Matt. 20:28). "Who gave himself as a ransom for all" (1 Tim. 2:6). "And the bread which I shall give for the life of the world is my flesh" (John 6:51). Then he adds, "Unless you eat the flesh of the Son of man and drink his blood, you have no life in you" (v. 53). Here salvation is available only to those who receive it through Christ's death.

"Since, therefore, we are now justified by his blood, much more shall we be saved by him from the wrath of God" (Rom. 5:9). "In whom we have redemption, the forgiveness of sins" (Col. 1:14). "You were ransomed from the futile ways inherited from your fathers, not with perishable things such as silver and gold, but with the precious blood of Christ, like that of a lamb without blemish or spot" (1 Pet. 1:18– 19). "But if we walk in the light, as he is in the light, we have fellowship with one another, and the blood of Jesus his Son cleanses us from all sin" (1 John 1:7). "To him who loves us, and has freed us from our sins by his blood" (Rev. 1:5). "Thou wast slain and by thy blood didst ransom men for God" (5:9). "They have washed their robes and made them white in the blood of the Lamb" (7:14).[5]

Upon this scriptural basis we behold God's plan for our salvation. However, our free moral choice must be considered in accepting or rejecting "so great salvation." The call of Christ to redemption is given freely to everyone. "Come to me, all who labor and are heavy laden, and I will give you rest" (Matt. 11:28) is universally extended but the decision is with the individual person.

1. *Conviction* produced by the Holy Spirit is sometimes referred to as a spiritual awakening. Through the Word of God the Holy Spirit speaks to us individually, awakening us to our need for salvation (Heb. 4:12).

2. Having recognized the need for salvation, individuals who are aware of this guilt weighing

upon their soul must *desire to be saved* (Acts 16:30). There must be a willingness to meet the conditions of the Bible.

3. *Godly sorrow* reveals the desire of the unsaved to be forgiven. It is the inward awareness that without God's forgiveness we are eternally lost. It is a deep sense of regret for the wrongs committed. "For godly grief produces a repentance that leads to salvation and brings no regret, but worldly grief produces death" (2 Cor. 7:10).

4. When one desires to be saved, it is determined by the individual's willingness to *repent.* Repentance is a sense of personal guilt, of grief for sins committed, hatred toward sin, and a determined turning away from it. Foremost in our understanding of repentance is that of forsaking sin. (See Acts 3:19; Isaiah 55:7; Psalm 51:17.)

5. Most difficult for some is the act of *confession.* Without this openness with God and ourselves there can be no real peace. "He who conceals his transgressions will not prosper, but he who confesses and forsakes them will obtain mercy" (Prov. 28:13). First John 1:9 informs us that the confession is to be made to the Lord. "If we confess our sins, he is faithful and just, and will forgive our sins." But it is also essential that we effect reconciliation with others as we confess to people whom we may have wronged (Acts 24:16; Matt. 5:23–24).

6. Confession to God often reveals areas of our lives in which we need to make *restitution.* In some situations reconciliation comes about through confession, asking forgiveness, or making an apology. However, in other instances it is necessary to pay

21

back what has been wrongfully taken from another. The repentant sinner desires to set right all that can be corrected. When such restitution is altogether impossible, it is the humble attitude of the heart that is recognized by the God of all grace (Luke 19:8)

7. *Forgiveness* is a two-way street! God's forgiveness of our sin is dependent upon our willingness to forgive others who may have wronged us individually (Matt. 6:14, 15). It is the attitude of Jesus expressed on the cross toward those who crucified him. Forgiveness leaves no room for malice, hatred, bitterness, or ill will. God's love will also enable us to forgive ourselves, thus bringing healing to our emotions.

8. Having allowed the Holy Spirit to bring conviction that results in godly sorrow, thus producing repentance that results in restitution and forgiveness, one must now *believe*. Through believing faith we claim God's plan of salvation as we obey the Word. For, "If you confess with your lips that Jesus is Lord and believe in your heart that God raised him from the dead, you will be saved. For man believes with his heart and so is justified, and he confesses with his lips and so is saved" (Rom. 10:9–10).

Salvation is God's gift to the believer. However, our continuing walk with the Lord is dependent upon our obedience to his Word. Those who teach the "eternal security of the believer" fail to read the complete text in John 10. To capture the complete thought one must read the entire passage. "My sheep hear my voice, and I know them, *and they follow me:* and I give them eternal life, and they shall never perish, and no one shall snatch them out of my hand. My Father, which gave them to me, is greater than all; and no one is able to snatch them out of the Father's hand" (vv. 27–29, italics added). Our security in Christ is determined by our personal obedience in following Christ. If we walk in the light as he is in the light, then we have fellowship with him. But if we reject the light of truth, then we walk in darkness, and how great is that darkness. In Christ we are not only saved but we are also constantly being saved as we walk the Highway of Holiness with him.

Questions for Study, Chapter 3

1. What was the purpose of Christ's coming into the world?
   (See Luke 19:10; Matthew 1:21.)

   _____

   _____

   _____

2. Explain in your own words the meaning of the atonement in God's plan of redemption. (See Matthew 20:28; Ephesians 1:7.)

   _____

   _____

   _____

3. In what manner is "free moral choice" exercised in salvation? (See 1 John 1:7; Matthew 11:28.) _____

   _____

   _____

   _____

4. Our awareness or conviction of sin is produced in what way? (See Hebrews 4:12; John 16:8–11.) _____

   _____

   _____

5. What is the difference between "remorse" for sin and "repentance" of sin? (See 2 Corinthians 7:10; Acts 3:19.) _____

_____

6. To whom and in what manner do we confess our sins? (See 1 John 1:9; Matthew 5:23 – 24.)_____

_____

7. Explain what *restitution* means? (See Luke 19:8.) _____

_____

Memorize:

> If you confess with your lips that Jesus is Lord and believe in your heart that God raised him from the dead, you will be saved. For man believes with his heart and so is justified, and he confesses with his lips and so is saved.
>
> —Romans 10:9–10

Chapter 4

Personhood: Created New in Christ

While salvation technically means "to save" or to heal, make sound, or preserve from death, other scriptural terms convey the meaning of "new life." The words of Jesus to Nicodemus were "Ye must be born again" (John 3:7). Through the exercising of free moral choice, the human will chooses to reject sin and believe in the resurrected Christ, thus producing a new life. Paul expressed it, "Therefore if any one is in Christ, he is a new creation; the old has passed away, behold, the new has come" (2 Cor. 5:17). It is compared in Scripture as being raised from the dead. The old life of sin is behind you, cast as far as the East is from the West to be remembered against you no more (Ps. 103:12). Truly, you have come into a new personhood in Christ.

27

Though saved instantly through faith, one must now apply that faith to living this new life. Salvation has accentuated our uniqueness as new persons in the image of Christ. Not all Christians are alike. Becoming a Christian only frees you to be the person God wants you to be. Peter emphasizes that we, "like newborn babes, long for the pure spiritual milk [of the Word], that by it [we] may grow up to salvation" (1 Pet. 2:2). Strength to live this new life comes from the Word of God and our obedience to that truth. Not only does it build strong spiritual convictions; it also enables you to "give an answer to every man that asketh you a reason of the hope that is in you with meekness and fear" (1 Pet. 3:15). During this formative period of your new life you are more receptive to the leadership of the Holy Spirit. Obedience to God's Word will help you to remain stable in time of the contrary winds. As Paul wrote, "Be no more children, tossed to and fro, and carried about with every wind of doctrine, by the sleight of men, and cunning craftiness, whereby they lie in wait to deceive; But speaking the truth in love, may grow up into him in all things, which is the head, even Christ" (Eph. 4:14–15).

Being a new creation does not conform us to all of the traditions of past history. The Galatian letter accentuates the fact that we are free from the religious teachings that others would impose upon us. "Stand fast therefore in the liberty wherewith Christ hath made us free, and be not entangled again with the yoke of bondage" (Gal. 5:1). Having been set free from sin, we are now free to be led of the Holy Spirit in conforming to God's plan for our lives.

Jesus stated that we are to be in the world but not of the world (John 17:14—16). Christians are a part of the community and culture in which they live this new life. Jesus was not an isolationist. He touched the lives of the common and ordinary persons of his day, giving them new life and principles by which to live. God has entrusted us with freedom to discipline our lives according to the principles set forth in the Bible—principles of integrity and decency in personal conduct. Some areas of conduct were very specifically dealt with. Those who were addicted to lying or stealing are admonished to cease because they are now living a new life in Christ. Their bodies and minds have become God's and his will controls their lives.

Four simple questions based upon biblical principles can be of great help in personal discipline as new persons in Christ.

1. Is this act constructive or destructive?
   (1 Cor. 10:23)

2. Does this produce bondage or liberty?
   (1 Cor. 6:12)

3. Is this to the glory of God or for my self-satisfaction?
   (1 Cor. 10:31)

4. Will this help or hinder other persons?
   (1 Cor. 8:9)

As unique persons we live in relationship to others and we must always be sensitive to how our personal freedom affects them. For that reason the

Word of God states, "Do not use your freedom as an opportunity for the flesh, but through love be servants of one another. For the whole law is fulfilled in one word, you shall love your neighbor as yourself" (Gal. 5:13 – 14).

Questions for Study, Chapter 4

1. Is salvation instantaneous or is it a process?
   (See Acts 16:30– 32; 2 Peter 3:18.)

   _____

   _____

2. What does the word *salvation* technically mean?

   _____

3. Salvation is also compared to what?
   (See Ephesians 2:5– 6.) _____

4. What do you believe Paul is referring to as the "old" that has passed away?
   (See 2 Corinthians 5:17.) _____

   _____

5. Explain in your own words how Christians can be different from one another and still serve Christ.
   (See Acts 15:36– 41; Romans 14.)

   _____

   _____

   _____

6. Outline for yourself a plan for daily Bible study to maintain this new life in Christ.
   (See 2 Timothy 2:15; 1 Peter 2:2.)

7. Discuss the Pauline principles in First Corinthians as possible aids to personal decision-making and value systems in today's world. Are they applicable?
   (See 1 Corinthians 10:23; 6:12; 10:31; 8:9.) _____

Memorize:

Therefore if any man be in Christ, he is a new creature: old things are passed away; behold, all things are become new.
                    —2 Corinthians 5:17

Chapter 5

Unity: Our Oneness in Christs

A^s "new persons" in Christ through the experience of being born again, we have become members of the family of God, and thus united to all other believers in Christ. "We are members one of another" (Eph. 4:25). Where sin had produced alienation, there is now reconciliation, wholeness, harmony, and unity. The psalmist expressed it as inspired of God, "Behold, how good and pleasant it is when brothers dwell in unity!" (133:1). Such unity is not that of the humanly organized institutional or denominational church, but the unity made possible through the lordship of Christ, a universal oneness.

True unity always finds its expression in the context of community and is lived out in relationship. In so doing, the spiritual moves into the realm of practical and experiential. The acceptance of Christ and obedience to his Word leaves no allowance for division of people by race, creed, culture, or sex. We have become one in Christ! "In Christ Jesus you who once were far off have been brought near in the blood of Christ. For he is our peace, who has made us both one, and has broken down the dividing wall of hostility" (Eph. 2:13– 14). This unity exceeded the cultural divisions existing between Jew, Gentile, and Greek at the time it was written. "There is neither Jew nor Greek, there is neither slave nor free, there is neither male nor female; for you are all one in Christ Jesus" (Gal. 3:28).

Scriptural unity is not unanimity nor does it happen automatically. As believers in Christ and his example of life, we desire to see this unity develop with other believers. Human relationships can be extremely difficult, even among believers. We have come to Christ from different backgrounds and with a variety of circumstances, as well as emotional differences. Our love for Christ and one another gives cohesiveness to the family of God. This is why Paul wrote, "With all lowliness and meekness, with patience, forbearing one another in love, eager to maintain the unity of the Spirit in the bond of peace" (Eph. 4:2– 3). Only in such an attitude can we serve him cooperatively while allowing for diversity without division.

Division is contrary to God's plan and purpose for his people. It is a serious offense to precipitate, participate in, or perpetuate acts that produce division. "Mark them which cause divisions and offenses contrary to the doctrine which ye have learned; and avoid them" (Rom. 16:17). Such conduct was viewed by Paul as being an indication of immaturity, an expression of our fleshly desires. "For ye are yet carnal: for whereas there is among you envying, and strife, and divisions, are ye not carnal, and walk as men?" (1 Cor. 3:3). While our human nature and constitutional makeup produces the potential for division, God's grace in the human heart enables us to live and work together in harmony that becomes our message of holiness.

Jesus prayed that we "may be one" as he and the Father are one (John 17:11). "There is one body and one Spirit" (Eph. 4:4), thus indicating the organic oneness revealed through purpose, activity, and mission in the world. The imagery used in the New Testament is that of a physical body functioning in a healthy manner with each part contributing to the success of the whole. "For as we have many members in one body, and all members have not the same office: so we, being many, are one body in Christ, and every one members one of another" (Rom. 12:4–5). Thus our unity is inclusive of all who are believers in Christ. Having received this truth, we are responsible to initiate action by reaching out to all others who have come to know Christ in the forgiveness of sin.

An all-inclusive, universal Church must of necessity transcend denominational labels, sectarian separateness, and geographical boundaries. Therefore, we seek to express our common faith by

35

uniting in worship and witness with other Christians. On the local level this can be evidenced by participation in community church ministries of evangelism and social concern. Our missionary endeavors around the world, on the other hand, make us aware that we can do together what we could never accomplish independently. As children of God we are interdependent, needing one another to fulfill Christ's prayer for unity.

Perfecting this unity will require more than human effort. In obedience to the Word of God these helpful guidelines emerge:

1. We are to be "in Christ"—which signifies salvation from sin—not of the world.

2. We must receive the Word of God and live by it, which requires the rejection of contrary doctrines of persons. "They have kept thy word" (John 17:6).

3. We are to be kept in the Father's name alone. "Holy Father, keep through thine own name those whom thou hast given me, that they may be one, as we are" (John 17:11).

4. We are to be sanctified wholly, enabling us to allow the Holy Spirit to cleanse us from those things that would divide.[6]

Yes, God's plan is for unity among all believers, and as obedient children we seek to live in that spirit of harmony.

Questions For Study, Chapter 5

1. What is the common belief that makes the people of God "one body"?
(See Ephesians 2:13–14; 4:25.)___

2. Does Christian unity remove all differences and individual opinion?
(See Romans 14.) _____

3. What does division within the body of Christ indicate about the parties involved?
(See 1 Corinthians 3:3)._____

4. When the unity of the Church is divided, how should this be handled by the community of faith?
(See Ephesians 4:2–3; Romans 16:17.) _____

5. Each member is vital to the proper functioning of the body. How did Paul explain this in 1 Corinthians 12:14–27?

_____

_____

6. Unity desired must be developed at the local and worldwide level. Give examples of each. _____

_____

7. Requirements for unity in John 17 can be stated in four New Testament truths.
John 17:16_____
John 17:6 _____
John 17:11_____
John 17:19_____

Memorize:

> For as we have many members in one body, and all members have not the same office: so we, being many, are one body in Christ, and everyone members one of another.
> —Romans 12:4—5

Chapter 6

The Church: God's People

The Church is a New Testament institution. The word *church* (including the plural form, *churches*) is used more than one hundred times in the New Testament, and it is referred to many more times. The first recorded use of the word is in Matthew 16:18, where Jesus said, "On this rock I will build my church, and the powers of death shall not prevail against it."

During Christ's earthly ministry he prepared for the Church, and from the Day of Pentecost on we find in actual existence a body of people who had been called out of sin and united in Christ. These believers were called "Christians" (Acts 11:26) and steadfastly followed the teachings of Christ and his apostles. So strong was their commitment to Christ and to one another that the believers "had all things common; and sold their possessions and goods, and parted them to all men as every man had need. And they, continuing daily with one accord in the temple, and breaking bread from house to house, did eat their meat with gladness and singleness of heart, praising God, and having favour with all the people. And the Lord added to the church daily such as should be saved" (Acts 2:44–47). This divine demonstration of commitment turned the world upside down (Acts 17:6).

Various figures of speech make plain the New Testament idea of the Church. It is a flock (John 10), all of one fold, following the Shepherd. It is the family of God (Eph. 3:15), composed of all who have been born again. It is a city whose inhabitants are all saved and recorded in the Lamb's Book of Life (Heb. 12:22). It is a house or building (1 Tim. 3:15) comprised of "living stones . . . built into a spiritual house" (1 Pet. 2:5), "joined . . . and built into it for a dwelling place of God in the Spirit" (Eph. 2:21–22). It is the Bride of Christ (Eph. 5:23–32; Rev. 21:9), pure, devoted, loyal. It is like a human body, a fitting symbol of its unity, symmetrical beauty, mutual helpfulness, and perfect organization. (See Romans 12:4–8 and 1 Corinthians 12.)

As "God's building" the Church is founded upon a "rock." It is "built upon the foundation of the apostles and prophets, Christ Jesus himself being the cornerstone" (Eph. 2:20). So the Church is not founded upon any person or group of persons nor upon human dogma or creeds, nor upon some person's idea or ideal, but on Christ himself. "No other foundation can any one lay than that which is laid, which is Jesus Christ" (1

Cor. 3:11). While history gives recognition to the prophets of old, John the baptizer, and later reformers in the Christian faith, *Christ alone* is the true foundation upon which the Church ultimately stands.

The Church is the body of Christ; hence it is only natural that he should be the head of his own body. He is "head over all things for the church, which is his body" (Eph. 1:22–23). "He is head of the body, the church" (Col. 1:18). The clarity of this Bible truth leaves no room for human systems that seek to establish earthly headquarters and leaders of the Church. If there is only one body, there can be only one head; and if there is only one head, then there is only one body.

As head of the Church, Christ was concerned about the name his bride would bear. Therefore in John 17:11 he prays, "Holy Father, keep them *in thy name* which thou hast given me, that they may be one, even as we are one" (italics added). His desire was that the Church be called by one name, and the name does make a difference. The family of God is not without a name; it bears the Father's own. Numerous times in the New Testament the writers designate the Bible name for the Church. (See 1 Corinthians 1:2; 10:32; 11:22; 15:9; 2 Corinthians 1:2, Galatians 1:13; 1 Timothy 3:5.) While out of respect some have named their churches after significant human leaders, the biblical name is *"the church of God,* which he hath purchased with his own blood" (Acts 20:28, italics added), for he alone is worthy. "For this cause I bow my knees unto the Father of our Lord Jesus Christ, *of whom the whole family in heaven and earth is named*" (Eph. 3:14– 15, italics added). Periodically throughout history because of the stigma attached to the name, some have been tempted to change to a nomenclature more acceptable to local congregations. Geographical location or community participation does not change the name of the Church. Without question it is the Church of God, for it belongs to him alone, not to any earthly being.

Since the Church belongs to God, he alone is capable of establishing the rules of faith and obedience for its members. Within the Bible we discover this guideline, for "all scripture is inspired by God and profitable for teaching, for reproof, for correction, and for training in righteousness" (2 Tim. 3:16). No human creed contains all the Word. If a creed contained all the Word, it would not be a human creed, but the divine Word of God. If a creed contained less than this it would not be sufficient; if more, it would contain too much. Of one standard we may be certain. A holy God, who inspires a Holy Bible, expects a holy people (1 Pet. 1:15– 16). Holiness is the normal standard of conduct for God's Church.

Entrance into God's Church is much easier than some would believe. "I am the door," said Jesus (John 10:9). The door is not baptism, nor penance, but Christ. No person can make you a member of the Church; nor can the other members of the Body vote you in or out. We cannot join the Church, and we do not automatically become members because mother and father brought us up in the Church of God. We must be added to the Church by the Lord. (See Acts 2:47.) He adds

42

only the saved. He adds *all* the saved. Hence the members of the Church are all the saved people, all who have been born again. "Your names are written in heaven" (Luke 10:20); they are "written in the book of life" (Rev. 20:15). We may have our names on membership roles here on earth, but unless they are written in the book of life it will avail nothing. While being born again places you in the family of God as a member, participation in a local congregation is required to enjoy the blessings of the Church. Regular, consistent participation in a local fellowship of believers is essential to maintain a healthy spiritual life (Heb. 10:25).

Questions for Study, Chapter 6

1. Who established the first church? (See Matthew 16:18.) _____

2. List at least three characteristics of the young church in Acts 2:44– 47.

   _____

3. Upon whom was the Church founded? (See 1 Corinthians 3:11.)_____

4. Paul gave the analogy that the Church is the body of Christ. Who is the head of the Body, as mentioned in Colossians 1:18? _____

5. What is the name of the Church and why is it important? (See John 17:11; Acts 20:28.) ___

6. Since we have no creed or dicipline, what is the standard of biblical scholarship and conduct for the Church of God as put forth in 2 Timothy 3:16 and 1 Peter 1:15– 16?

   _____

7. How can you become a member of
   the Church of God?
   (See Acts 2:47.) _____

_____

Memorize:

> Upon this rock I will build my church; and
> the gates of hell shall not prevail against
> it.
> — Matthew 16:18

Chapter 7

The Holy Spirit: God's Gift

The Holy Spirit is the promised gift of our heavenly Father (Luke 24:49). In John 15 and 16 Jesus Christ reveals the nature of the Spirit. "When the Spirit of truth comes, he will guide you into all truth; for he will not speak on his own authority, but whatever he hears he will speak, and he will declare to you the things that are to come" (John 16:13).

The word *holy* means pure, morally and spiritually acceptable to God, consecrated for his purpose alone. That the Holy Spirit is a person is revealed in Scripture, which states that he has a will (1 Cor. 12:11), intelligence (Rom. 8:27), knowledge (1 Cor. 2:11–12), power (Acts 1:8), and a capacity for love (Rom. 15:30). In Acts 5:3–4, the Holy Spirit's interrelatedness to God is revealed. In Psalm 139:7–10 he is shown to be omnipresent, or in all places. John 14:2 teaches that he knows all things—that he has the attribute of omniscience. He is eternal with the Father and the Son, as shown in Hebrews 9:14. We can see, then, the importance and the significance that Jesus attached to the Holy Spirit (Luke 24:49).

The Holy Spirit is involved in the totality of our Christian experience.

1. *He convicts.* The Holy Spirit awakens the individual to an awareness of sin and constrains him or her to seek God's pardon. Without conviction no one would realize the need for salvation (John 1:8—11).

2. *He bears witness to our salvation* (Rom. 8:16). The Holy Spirit enables us to know when God accepts us into his family. This assurance will banish doubt and fear regarding our relationship to God.

3. *He regenerates. Regenerate* here means to renew the heart, causing one to respond to the love of God. That is what takes place when one is born again, and it is the Holy Spirit who effects the new birth (John 3:3,5). This is the most important transition in the New Testament so far as God and humanity are concerned. To be "born anew," or "born from above" (RSV marginal note, John 3:3) is the purpose of the whole plan of salvation. It is the beginning of spiritual life, and this life is brought about by the Holy Spirit.

4. *He guides* (John 16:13). There is a difference between a guide and a guidepost or map. A guide goes right with us, leading and counseling, assisting us in decisions to be made, as well as giving us directions we are to follow. Isaiah had

prophesied of a wonderful counselor, and the Holy Spirit both counsels and guides as we follow his leadership.

5. *He fills or baptizes* (Eph. 5:18; Acts 1:8). The importance of being filled with the Holy Spirit cannot be exaggerated. However, this experience is often misunderstood. The Bible stresses the manifestations and the demonstration of the Spirit more than the experience. The reason for this is clear; we can see a demonstration, but we have to be told about an experience. (Read 1 Corinthians 2:4; 12:7.)

6. *He glorifies Christ.* "He will glorify me" Jesus said (John 16:14). One manifestation of a Spirit-filled life is the preeminence given to Christ. A selfish person thinks of self first, and even tries to "use" the Spirit of God to exalt self. A Spirit-filled person is "used" by the Spirit, and the interests of the kingdom of God predominate.

7. *He translates or interprets.* "He will take what is mine and declare it to you" (John 16:14). We would never be able to understand or appropriate the work of Christ unless the Holy Spirit imparted the knowledge to our own hearts. The unbeliever cannot comprehend the mystery of Calvary; indeed it appears to be foolishness until the Holy Spirit reveals the purpose of it (1 Cor. 2:14– 16).

8. *He imparts gifts* (1 Cor. 12:3– 11). You will observe how various gifts are dispensed according to the all-wise determination of the Spirit. We should seek to use our gifts fully and always for the glory of Christ. In seeking to be filled with the Holy Spirit, we should always be in an attitude to receive whatever gift he may wish to impart.

9. *He helps our prayer life* (Rom. 8:26– 27). Spirit-filled people are people of prayer, and their prayers are effectual because the Holy Spirit interprets their hearts' desires to God, and God hears. Praying in the Spirit (Eph. 6:18) is the kind of praying that brings an answer. Romans 8:26 reveals the love the Holy Spirit bears toward honest seekers.

10. *He blesses our work for Christ.* Acts 2:41 tells of three thousand persons coming to Christ — the result of one sermon preached by Peter, who was filled with the Holy Spirit. So many lives are barren of spiritual power because they try performing supernatural deeds in their own strength instead of depending entirely upon the Holy Spirit.

11. *He warns us of spiritual dangers and pitfalls* (Isa. 30:21). If you listen, the Spirit will admonish you when you leave the right path. The same idea is contained in John 16:8: "He will convince . . . concerning sin and righteousness."

12. *He inspires.* The influence of the Holy Spirit made it possible for the writers of the Bible to prophesy and to reveal many truths impossible of discovery through natural means. He also enables true gospel workers to witness to the saving truth of that gospel.

Because the influence of the Holy Spirit is so necessary to our success in living the Christian life, God has given us three warnings: (1) We must not resist him (Acts 7:51). People who resist conviction and refuse to yield to God resist the Holy Spirit just as much as do those who oppose the gospel of Christ. It is a dangerous thing to do. (2) We are warned not to grieve the Holy Spirit

(Eph. 4:30). You can grieve only one you love or one who loves you. Every wrong deed, motive, or passion grieves the Holy Spirit, and he seeks to give us victory over all wickedness. (3) We are commanded not to quench the Holy Spirit (1 Thess. 5:19). That is, we must not obstruct or impede his work. Spiritual life is very sensitive; even an impure thought impairs it. A bad, uncontrolled temper kills it, and an unruly tongue ruins its influence.

The person who is filled with the Holy Spirit will manifest the same characteristics that the Holy Spirit has, namely, holiness of life, purity, sinlessness, unselfishness, and Christlikeness. If you remember how Jesus cleansed the Temple by driving out every unclean, sinful thing, you will have some idea of this attitude toward sin in one's heart. The heart is now the temple of God (1 Cor. 3:16), and the Holy Spirit must cleanse it in order to dwell there.[7]

Questions for Study, Chapter 7

1. The Holy Spirit is a person. Please list scriptural references that reveal these characteristics.
   He has a will._____
   He is intelligent. _____
   He has a capacity for love. _____
2. How are we made aware of our need for salvation?
   (See John 16:8 – 11.) _____

   _____

3. What assurance do we have in Romans 8:16 that we are saved?

   _____

   _____

4. Decisions of life — marriage, vocation, or others — are never easy. In what way does the Holy Spirit help us according to John 16:13 in this aspect of Christian living?

   _____

   _____

5. According to John 16:14, the Holy Spirit dwells within the believer for what purpose?

   _____

   _____

6. By what means does the Holy Spirit
   equip us to serve in the body of
   Christ?
   (See 1 Corinthians 12:4– 11.) ⎯⎯

7. As people of prayer, the Holy Spirit
   assists us in what manner?
   (See Romans 8:26– 27.) ⎯⎯⎯⎯

Memorize:

But ye shall receive power, after that the
Holy Ghost is come upon you: and ye shall
be witnesses unto me both in Jerusalem, and
in all Judaea, and in Samaria, and unto the
uttermost part of the earth.

—Acts 1:8

Chapter 8

Holiness: God's Nature in Us

Holiness is the very nature of God. It speaks of his transcendency over all creation, of his awesome glory, and his impeccable character. Through the inspired writers, God has revealed his desire that we, too, should share in his holiness. "For I am the Lord your God; consecrate yourselves therefore, and be holy, for I am holy" (Lev. 11:44). This same expectancy is proclaimed in 1 Peter: "But as he who called you is holy, be holy yourselves in all your conduct; since it is written, 'You shall be holy, for I am holy'" (1:15–16).

Basic to our understanding of holiness is the concept of wholeness or completeness that is possible only through yielding to the Holy Spirit. The extent of saving grace goes beyond the initial forgiveness of sin (conversion) to the sanctifying of our very nature through the infilling of the Holy Spirit. "He is able also to save them to the *uttermost* that come unto God by him" (Heb. 7:25, italics added). This scriptural truth challenges the "new person" to go on to experience the possibilities that have become ours through faith in Christ. "Therefore leaving the principles of the doctrine of Christ, let us go on unto perfection" (Heb. 6:1).

Without question, Paul affirmed that holiness was God's *will* for every believer (1 Thess. 4:3). We are called not only to regeneration but also to consecration and holiness (Rom. 12:1). This became the prayer of Paul as he wrote, "May the God of peace himself sanctify you wholly; and may your spirit and soul and body be kept sound and blameless at the coming of our Lord Jesus Christ" (1 Thess. 5:23). Biblical theology is more important in this matter than semantic terminology. Whether we use the term *entire sanctification*, *second-blessing holiness*, *Christian perfection*, or *perfect love*, we may be sure that there is a crisis experience in the Holy Spirit beyond that of initial conversion. This experience equips the child of God to live a life of holiness, revealing total commitment to the will of God and wholeness to life.

The term second work of grace implies that it is subsequent to or follows after regeneration. The disciples for whom Christ prayed (John 17:9) were already believers. And he addressed this same band of believers in Acts 1:8, "Ye shall receive power, after that the Holy Ghost is come upon you: and ye shall be witnesses." Salvation precedes the experience of Pentecost.

Acts 2:4 demonstrates the symbolism of fire accompanying the coming of the Holy Spirit on the Day of Pentecost. No actual fire being present, the symbol was intended to indicate the cleansing aspect of the Holy Spirit. This divine cleansing purges the attitudes and disposition of the believer until the image of Christ is reflected in him or her. All of our emotions are left fully intact but are cleansed and sensitized by the Holy Spirit. Nothing essentially human is removed in the sanctifying experience. One's ability to love, hate, laugh, and cry are now freed from the curse of sin to be experienced rightly as God's child. The believer now demonstrates the graces of the sanctified life as spoken of in Galatians 5:22 – 23: "But the fruit of the Spirit is love, joy, peace, patience, kindness, goodness, faithfulness, gentleness, self-control." Such holy disposition enables one to make full use of the gifts of the Spirit as spoken of in Romans 12, 1 Corinthians 12, and Ephesians 4. The gifts of the Spirit are not to be sought after, but rather we are to seek the person of the Holy Spirit. Then he will give the gifts of the Spirit "severally as he will" (1 Cor. 12:11). The gifts of the Spirit are always given for "the perfecting of the saints, for the work of ministry, for the edifying of the body of Christ" (Eph. 4:12). Nowhere in Scripture do we find that any of the gifts were used as criteria to indicate one's having received the Holy Spirit. Therefore, it is wrong to say that the gift of prophecy, the gift of tongues, or healing is necessary to authenticate the infilling or baptism

57

of the Holy Spirit. All of the gifts are given to edify the Church, never to cause division. The Spirit of the Holy Spirit is that of perfect love and the gifts are to be exercised in a decent and orderly manner (1 Cor. 14:40), thus glorifying God and edifying the Church. While the gifts listed in Scripture are not to be interpreted as exhaustive, they are indicative of how God gifts the Church, equipping her for the whole ministry entrusted to the community of faith.

Holiness is essential in the believer's life. We dare not treat this doctrine as an elective in religious studies. Jesus said, "Blessed are the pure of heart, for they shall see God" (Matt. 5:8). And the writer of Hebrews counsels us, "Strive for peace with all men, and for the holiness *without* which no one will see the Lord" (12:14, italics added).

Questions for Study, Chapter 8

1. The Christian is called to "go on" to perfection (Heb. 6:1). In your own words, explain what this means for the Christian. _____

   _____

   _____

2. *Sanctification* means to be "set apart for sacred use." Where do we find the basis for the doctrine of *entire* sanctification? Write out 1 Thessalonians 5:23 in your own words.

   _____

   _____

   _____

   _____

3. By a "second work of grace" we mean that before receiving the infilling of the Holy Spirit we must be what? (See John 3:7, 17:9.) ___

4. List four other terms used to indicate an experience of holiness. ___

   _____

   _____

   _____

   _____

5. The word *fire* in Scripture is often a symbol of cleansing. Is heart purity that which is external or internal? (See Ephesians 5:26 and 2 Corinthians 7:1.) _____

_____

_____

6. Does sanctification remove our emotions? If not, in what manner does the Holy Spirit help us? (See Galatians 5:22.)

_____

_____

7. What is the evidence of a truly Spirit-filled life as indicated in 1 Corinthians 12:31 — 13:1 — 13?_____

_____

_____

Memorize:

And the very God of peace sanctify you wholly; and I pray God your whole spirit and soul and body be preserved blameless unto the coming of our Lord Jesus Christ.
— 1 Thessalonians 5:23

Chapter 9

Stewardship: The Christian's Responsibility

Stewardship deals with all of life. It recognizes that God is the Creator and giver of "every good endowment and every perfect gift" (James 1:17). Implied in stewardship is the account we will give for the ways we have utilized the gifts that God has entrusted to our care. "It is required in stewards, that a man be found faithful" (1 Cor. 4:2). Every person will give an account for the way he or she has lived (2 Cor. 5:10).

Christian stewardship must always begin with this concept of "wholeness." The biblical base for this teaching is summed up in the words, "You shall love the Lord your God with all *your heart,* and with *all your soul,* and with *all your strength,* and with *all your mind;* and your neighbor as yourself" (Luke 10:27, italics added). When one becomes a Christian, God has claim on and control of his or her whole life.

The *physical body* entrusted to us is to be kept and used for the glory of God. "Do you know that your body is a temple of the Holy Spirit within you, which you have from God? You are not your own; you were bought with a price, so glorify God in your body" (1 Cor. 6:19– 20). In Christ we have been freed from the sins of the flesh and we have now become responsible to keep our physical bodies pure for his dwelling.

Christ being the Lord of our lives, we are accountable to him for the *possessions* entrusted to us. Material wealth of houses, lands, stocks and bonds, money, and all other earthly goods are to be safely guarded and liberally shared. Our willingness and ability to give are to be developed in a regular, consistent pattern of proportionate giving. "On the first day of every week, each of you is to put something aside and store it up, as he may prosper" (1 Cor. 16:2). This concept of stewardship in the financial realm helps us to see beyond the legalism of the tithe. Jesus used the tithe only as a base for the beginning of giving as an expression of love. "You tithe mint and rue and every herb, and neglect justice and the love of God; these you ought to have done, without neglecting the others" (Luke 11:42). Love prompts us to give liberally and consistently as we cheerfully serve the Lord (2 Cor. 9:7). Even the person with the least of this world's goods is able to give unto God (Luke 21:1– 4). Miserliness quenches the Spirit but regular giving to the local church and the worldwide mission of the Church produce blessings in abundance.

The *ability to think and reason* is also a trust from God. How we develop this potential and use it is a vital part of our stewardship, since it affects all of the others. We are to have a thoughtful approach to life as Christ did (Phil. 2:5), and we are admonished to "think" about the things that elevate life to the pure, positive, and holy (Phil. 4:8). Christian faith demands intellectual integrity. We are to develop our minds to better serve the Lord. "Study to shew thyself approved unto God, a workman that needeth not to be ashamed, rightly dividing the word of truth" (2 Tim. 2:15).

While we have dealt only with the physical, material, and mental, this in no way lessens our responsibility for the spiritual quality of our lives. Personal prayer habits, Bible study, witnessing, and worship are essential if we are to give an account for the soul that God has entrusted to each of us.

Questions For Study, Chapter 9

1. As a Christian we have a heightened awareness of God as creator. In your own words write out James 1:17. __
   _____
   _____
   _____

2. Stewardship implies a day of judgment or accountability. According to 2 Corinthians 5:10, will Christians have to give account for their use of life? _____
   _____
   _____

3. Luke 10:27 outlines our total surrender to God. List four areas specifically mentioned. _____
   _____
   _____

4. Does it make any difference how we abuse our bodies through drugs, overwork, or overeating? Why? (See 1 Corinthians 6:19– 20.) _____
   _____
   _____
   _____

5. According to 1 Corinthians 9:27, when saved do we automatically have bodies that glorify God, or must we exercise discipline?_____

_____

6. Is it sufficient, according to Luke 11:42 and 1 Corinthians 16:2, to give only a tithe in support of God's work? _____

_____

7. In what way are we accountable for our spiritual, mental, and social aspects of life? (See Philippians 4:8 and 2 Timothy 2:15.)

_____

_____

Memorize:

It is required in stewards, that a man be found faithful.

—1 Corinthians 4:2

Chapter 10

Ordinances: Instituted by Christ

The observance of ordinances in the New Testament church rests upon their institution by Christ and upon the last commission he gave to his apostles: "Go therefore and make disciples of all nations, baptizing them in the name of the Father and of the Son and of the Holy Spirit, teaching them to observe all that I have commanded you; and lo, I am with you always, to the close of the age" (Matt. 28:19–20). In this text, ordinances are expressly commanded and their observance is to be perpetuated "to the close of the age."

An *ordinance* has been defined as "an outward symbol divinely appointed to represent a great fact or truth of the gospel and the personal relation of the recipient to that fact or truth; a divine requirement, making its obligation universal and perpetual."[8] It is an act instituted by Christ, practiced by the early church, and taught in God's Word.

The student of God's Word recognizes that the ordinances are not the source of our salvation, or a test of fellowship. Our observance of and participation in the ordinances is a witness to our obedience to the teaching of God's Word and the example left by Christ for us to follow.

A Believer's Baptism

The last commission of Christ, as recorded by Mark, is this: "And he said to them, 'Go into all the world and preach the gospel to the whole creation. He who believes and is baptized will be saved; but he who does not believe will be condemned' " (Mark 16:15–16). These words clearly limit the subjects of baptism to those who are capable of hearing and believing the gospel, and this standard was invariably maintained by the apostles in their ministry. No children were baptized, but only persons who were capable of believing — "men and women" (Acts 8:12).

Peter taught the necessity of repentance first and baptism afterward: "Repent, and be baptized every one of you" (Acts 2:38). Unless the heart is brought into the right attitude through repentance, the simple act of baptism amounts to nothing, even if it is performed in the Bible manner and by a true minister of God.

Baptism is a ceremonial representation of the burial and resurrection of our Lord; therefore, only immersion is appropriate. In fact, the individual believer symbolically follows Christ in his death, burial, and resurrection. First the believer dies the death to sin, or is "crucified with Christ" (Gal. 2:20); then he or she is "buried with [Christ] in baptism." Colossians 2:12 goes on to indicate that the believer is raised with Christ through faith in the working of God, who raised Christ from the dead. Baptism thus becomes an outward sign to the individual of an inward work of grace.

This idea is alluded to in the remarkable passage in Romans 6:2,4. "How can we who died to sin still live in it? . . . We were buried therefore with him by baptism into death, so that as Christ was raised from the dead by the glory of the Father, we too might walk in newness of life." Christ was buried in baptism. John was baptizing "in the river Jordan" (Mark 1:5). "Then Jesus came from Galilee to the Jordan to John, to be baptized by him. . . . And when Jesus was baptized, he went up immediately from the water, and behold, the heavens were opened and he saw the Spirit of God descending like a dove, and alighting on him; and lo, a voice from heaven, saying, 'This is my beloved Son, with whom I am well pleased' " (Matt. 3:13, 16— 17). Jesus went down into the Jordan in order to be baptized, for after his baptism, he "went up straightway out of the water." Here we have the highest authority for immersion in water: (1) *Jesus himself,* the Son of God, set the example (that of itself should be sufficient); (2) *the Holy*

Spirit, the third person in the Trinity, bore witness by appearing visibly in the form of a dove and lighting upon Christ; (3) *the Father* declared in audible tones, "I am well pleased."

In order to fulfill the Word of God perfectly and secure a valid baptism, the candidate must observe the following:

1. *He or she must know or hear the gospel* (Mark 16:15).

2. *He or she must repent of his or her sins and believe the gospel,* the doing of which will bring about salvation (Acts 3:19; 16:31; 2:38).

3. *The believer must find a minister of God who is ready to baptize him or her* (See Acts 8:36—37.)

4. *Preacher and candidate must go to a place where there is "much water"* (John 3:23).

5. *Then he or she must follow the example of Christ* in his baptism (Matt. 3:16), by going down "into the water." (See Acts 8:38.)

6. *Then he or she must be "buried . . . in baptism"* (Col. 2:12).

7. *The candidate can then come "up out of the water"* (Acts 8:39).

8. Then, having obeyed the Word and followed the Lord, *he or she can go "on his [or her] way rejoicing"* (Acts 8:39).

Baptism as an ordinance does not cleanse the soul from sin actually, but ceremonially, serving as "a testimony unto them"—the people. It is the outward sign of an inward work of grace. We have "died to sin" and are therefore "buried . . . with him by baptism" (Rom. 6:2,4). The actual cleansing of the soul from sinful elements cannot be effected by literal water; only "the blood of Christ"

70

is able to "purify your conscience from dead works to serve the living God" (Heb. 9:14). Christ "has freed us from our sins by his blood" (Rev. 1:5). "The blood of Jesus his Son cleanses us from all sin" (1 John 1:7).

The Lord's Supper

The New Testament also teaches the observance of an ordinance called "the Lord's Supper." This expression, however, is used only once: "When you meet together, it is not the Lord's supper that you eat" (1 Cor. 11:20).

Paul then proceeded to show what the true Lord's Supper really is. "For I received from the Lord what I also delivered to you, that the Lord Jesus on the night when he was betrayed took bread, and when he had given thanks, he broke it, and said, 'This is my body which is broken for you. Do this in remembrance of me.' In the same way also the cup, after supper, saying, 'This cup is the new covenant in my blood. Do this, as often as you drink it, in remembrance of me.' For as often as you eat this bread and drink the cup, you proclaim the Lord's death until he comes" (1 Cor. 11:23–26).

According to the Apostle, the Lord's Supper is the eating of the bread and the drinking of the cup, after the example set by Christ. Therefore, the Lord's Supper and Communion are the same (1 Cor. 10:16).

Paul states that this ordinance was instituted by Christ. "Now as they were eating, Jesus took bread, and blessed, and broke it, and gave it to the disciples and said, 'Take, eat; this is my body.'

71

And he took a cup, and when he had given thanks he gave it to them, saying, 'Drink of it, all of you; for this is my blood of the covenant, which is poured out for many for the forgiveness of sins' " (Matt. 26:26–28).

To be rightly understood the Lord's Supper must be viewed in the Jewish setting of Passover. Here the Jews recall their deliverance from Egypt and the sacrificial Paschal lamb (Exod. 12). As a people they remember their bondage, being reminded that the blood of the lamb applied to their door posts had set them free, and as God commanded, they took only unleavened bread.

In this context the followers of Christ participate in the Lord's Supper, remembering "the Lamb of God, which taketh away the sin of the world" (John 1:29). Through Christ's death on the cross we have participated in "the blood of the everlasting covenant" (Heb. 13:20). Never again need another die, for Christ has set us free. We are to remember this as we receive the fruit of the vine and the unleavened bread. Each time, we recall that "without shedding of blood is no remission" of sin (Heb. 9:22). Only through faith in the Christ whose body was broken and whose blood was shed for our salvation are we delivered from sin.

Following the example and commandment of Christ, the apostolic church observed this ordinance (Acts 20:7). The testimony of the earliest church leaders is that the ordinance of Communion was observed regularly by all Christians; and the observance has continued among Christians until the present day.

While observed each Lord's Day by some churches, no specific requirement is established in the New Testament. But as often as you do it, do it in remembrance of Christ with a sense of reverence in worship.

Foot Washing

As a Christian ordinance, foot washing symbolizes, as does nothing else, the sacredness and holiness of that blessed *relationship of God's redeemed saints with one another* and their servanthood role in the world.

If spiritual separation from the world as a distinct act of God's grace demands outward expression and exhibition in Christian baptism, and if the moral and inner secret of regeneration through the atonement and our abiding life in Christ calls for outward and frequent expression in the literal observance of the Lord's Supper, then — and equally true and important — that inner and spiritual person-to-person relationship calls for a corresponding outward expression such as Christ himself instituted when he said, "Wash one another's feet" (John 13:14).

As we have seen, Christ himself set the example, instituted the practice, and then commanded its observance. That is sufficient to establish it; for it is exactly the same method by which the other two ordinances were established.

"You call me Teacher and Lord; and you are right, for so I am. If I then, your Lord and Teacher, have washed your feet, you also ought to wash one another's feet. For I have given you an example, that you also should do as I have done to you. . . . If you know these things, blessed are you if you do them" (John 13:13–17).

The ordinance of foot washing, like the other ordinances, is intended to teach us some important lessons. It teaches a lesson of humility, made very clear to us when we practice it. It also sets forth our position of equality in the Church, showing that we all, as brothers and sisters, belong on the same common level. Jesus himself, our Lord and Master, humbled himself and washed the feet of his disciples; therefore, how much more reasonable it is that we should wash one another's feet. It also shows that we are properly a servant people, and that we must minister to the good of others.[9]

Questions for Study, Chapter 10

1. Please define the meaning of an *ordinance* in the Church.

   _____

   _____

   _____

2. Are we saved by observing the ordinances? (See John 1:12 and Acts 16:31). _____

   If not, then why do we observe these ordinances in God's Church?

   _____

   _____

3. Baptism is by _____ pouring, _____ immersion, _____ sprinkling? (See Matthew 3:13–17 and Colossians 2:12.)

   What is the symbolism of this experience? _____

   _____

   _____

4. Infant baptism is not taught in the Bible (Acts 8:12). What, according to Romans 10:9, is the error of the practice of infant baptism?

   _____

   _____

5. In the Lord's Supper we use two elements: the fruit of the vine and unleavened bread. What do these two elements symbolize? (See 1 Corinthians 11:23–26.) _____

6. Participation in the service of Communion is a serious time of heart searching, not a time for mere ritual. To drink unworthily carries severe penalty. According to 1 Corinthians 11:28–29, what is it?

7. Give the scriptural reference for the ordinance of foot washing. _____ What is the symbolic meaning of this teaching? _____

Memorize:

> Go therefore and make disciples of all nations . . . teaching them to observe all that I have commanded you.
>
> —Matthew 28:19–20

Chapter 11

Divine Healing: Available through Christ

Divine healing and belief in its reality are reasonable on the ground of the divine promises that are expressed or implied in the Scriptures. These promises are of two main classes — general and specific. General promises are those made concerning whatever one may ask. Specific promises are those that offer something on certain conditions. Examples of general promises are as follows: "And whatever you ask in prayer, you will receive" (Matt. 21:22). "Whatever you ask in prayer, you will receive, if you have faith" (Mark 11:24). "Ask whatever you will, and it shall be done for you" (John 15:7). "If you ask anything of the Father, he will give it to you" (John 16:23). If these were the only promises of answers to prayer

77

for the sick, they alone would furnish sufficient ground for belief in divine healing.

The specific promises of healing are very definite. In the Great Commission as recorded by Mark, Jesus said that other signs of healing would follow his earthly ministry. Mark wrote, "They will lay their hands on the sick, and they will recover" (16:18). The healing of the sick promised here was not to be done through the apostles, but through those to whom the apostles were commanded to preach and who chose to believe.

Both salvation and healing are included in the Great Commission. A question has sometimes been raised as to the genuineness of this verse, but it is found in all but one of the four oldest Greek manuscripts and is generally accepted by textual critics. Though Matthew's record of the Great Commission does not specifically promise healing, it is implied in the words "teaching them to observe all that I have commanded you." Jesus taught the apostles to pray for healing and commissioned them to teach others to do so, which implies his intention to answer such prayers.

The gifts of healing are represented in 1 Corinthians 12:9–30 as common in the Church at the time Paul wrote. He points out that they belong not merely to apostles but to whomsoever God might be pleased to give them. From these gifts of healing we might infer the fact of healing. No promise of healing is more specific than that given in James 5:14, 15: "Is any among you sick? Let him call for the elders of the church, and let them pray over him, anointing him with oil in the name of the Lord; and the prayer of faith will save the

78

sick man, and the Lord will raise him up; and if he has committed sins, he will be forgiven." The power to heal, according to this scripture, belongs not merely to the apostles who would soon pass away, but to the Church as a whole.

Divine healing is physical healing by divine power directly manifested in answer to prayer and faith. Because God is the author of nature and imminent in nature and his power is back of all its operations, all healing resulting from natural processes is in a sense divine healing. One may properly give thanks to God for such healing. Though healing comes through the use of natural remedies, it may be attributed to God, who has created all those things and given them whatever beneficial qualities they possess.

But none of these natural processes is divine healing in the sense that the Scriptures use it. Divine healing is not natural, but supernatural healing. It is a miraculous manifestation that transcends nature. Though it affects the material body, it does not take place by material means. As to its mode, it is like the new birth of which Jesus said, "The wind blows where it wills, and you hear the sound of it, but you do not know whence it comes or whither it goes; so it is with everyone who is born of the Spirit" (John 3:8). Likewise mysterious is the mode of God in the work of supernatural healing.

Though God's will is generally to heal the sick, he is more concerned about spiritual and moral excellence than about physical health; therefore, God may allow us to go through periods of suffering. Thus, healing is not parallel with salvation.

God's will is always to save the soul, though not always to heal the body.

Divine healing may be either instantaneous or gradual. It seems probable the healings recorded in the Bible were nearly all, if not all, instantaneous. Of all the healings described in the New Testament, the fact that any were accomplished gradually cannot be positively shown. Because those healings were told in order to show the power of God, it was important that only instantaneous healings be recorded. But the Bible does not state that God did not then or will not now sometimes heal gradually. Neither is there any rational ground for excluding gradual healing by divine power. Many persons today are healed in answer to prayer. This is reason enough for believing that God will heal in this manner. To say an instance of healing is gradual is not to say it is indefinite or unreal. One may definitely begin to recover at a particular time from a disease of many years and in a few days' time be completely restored. Such healings are not instantaneous but gradual; yet they are real.

Also, healing may be either partial or complete, or it may be either temporary or permanent and yet be genuine divine healing. Jesus once healed a blind man by two distinct stages. Not infrequently persons today receive partial healing in answer to prayer. Sometimes such persons receive complete healing later; in other instances they do not. Others are temporarily restored and soon after become afflicted again in the same manner. Many, however, are instantly and completely healed.

The classical text on divine healing is James 5:13–18. There the Church is commanded to anoint the sick with oil in the name of the Lord and pray over them. Such anointing was practiced by Jesus' disciples in their healing of the sick: "So they went out and preached that men should repent. And they cast out many demons, and *anointed with oil* many that were sick and healed them" (Mark 6:12,13, italics added). What is the purpose of this anointing of the sick with oil? The oil in itself has no curative value when merely placed upon the head. Olive oil was commonly used for purposes of anointing. In special instances a costly perfume was used either mixed with the oil or alone as in the anointing of Jesus at Bethany. But in no case did the oil possess special healing properties. Oil is represented in the Scriptures as symbolic of the Holy Spirit. The anointing of the sick with oil signifies the Spirit and the power of God coming upon the sick to heal them. It is a very apt symbol and is therefore helpful to the faith of those afflicted. It is also an act of obedience, the practice of which helps to give definiteness and strength to one's faith.

Similar in purpose to anointing of the sick is the laying on of hands in prayer for the healing of the sick. Jesus and the apostles often laid their hands upon the sick or touched them in order to heal them. The laying on of hands by those who are called to pray for the sick is a symbolic conveying of divine power, much as there was a giving of the Holy Ghost by the laying of the apostles' hands upon believers.

There is no reason for believing the power of God is actually transmitted by the laying on of hands or that it might not come upon the sick person as well without this physical contact. But as a symbolic transmission of divine power to the body of the suffering one, it has much value in assisting the sick person to believe, and in making real to his or her consciousness the fact of the divine operation in healing.

The conditions for healing are few and simple. The primary and all-important condition is faith. Unbelief at Nazareth hindered the performance of many mighty works there. The disciples failed to cure the demoniac son because of their unbelief. Jesus said to one who questioned his ability, "All things are possible to him who believes" (Mark 9:23). In James 5:15 we read, "The prayer of faith shall save the sick." The faith necessary to healing is not a mere theoretical or intellectual belief in God's power, but a trustful and confident stepping out on the divine promise as it applies to the present need. It is a bold reliance upon God to heal a particular ailment at a particular time. Faith is not a mere arbitrary requirement for healing. Faith is that which connects God's healing with the consciousness of the one who prays.[10]

Questions for Study, Chapter 11

1. Jesus taught by the example of healing the sick. Select one of the following passages and share the specific story with someone else: Mark 9:14– 29; Luke 14:1– 4; John 4:43– 53.
2. Some believe that divine healing ceased with the apostles. Using the following texts, explain why this is not true: James 5:14,15; 1 Corinthians 12:9– 30. _____

   _____

3. If you were asked to explain what you mean by divine healing, how would you state it and support it with Scripture?

   _____

   _____

   _____

4. Not everyone is healed—does this mean that those who are not have insufficient faith? Discuss this with a friend after reading 2 Corinthians 12:7– 10. Record your reactions.

   _____

   _____

5. Mark 6:12,13 and James 5:14 mention anointing with oil when praying for the sick. Is there healing virtue in the oil? What is the purpose of this act?_____

_____

_____

7. If you are sick and need healing, what does James 5:14 teach you to do?_____

_____

Memorize:

And Jesus went about . . . healing every sickness and every disease among the people.
— Matthew 9:35

Chapter 12

Ministry: The Christian's Opportunity

The Great Commission (Matt. 28:19– 20) places both an opportunity and a responsibility before the believer in Christ. Our new life in Christ is for the purpose of *service*, even as our Master came to minister to human need (Matt. 20:28). As exemplified in Jesus' own ministry, *prayer* becomes primary in preparing for service (Mark 1:35) and in fulfilling his plan. "Pray ye therefore the Lord of the harvest, that he will send forth laborers into his harvest" (Matt. 9:38). More than a spiritual exercise, prayer is the indispensable ingredient in the Christian life and witness. It is the first requirement in being adequately prepared for any role of service in God's Church.

The priesthood of all believers affords the opportunity for every Christian to serve in some significant ministry. The Bible knows no designation such as clergy and laity, for we have all become "kings and priests unto God" (Rev. 1:6). Every believer is a minister in the New Testament meaning of the word. We have become a "royal priesthood" as stated in 1 Peter 2:9, thus giving to each person a direct access to God's grace and power. As such, we are expected to be involved in the continuing ministry of the Church, exercising the gifts that God has given to us. Such a ministry will require maturity of both pastor and people, recognizing that each has a unique contribution to make in ministry. Where the Holy Spirit predominates we should be able to accept one another and not be threatened by the ability of other members of the Body.

Evangelism, or the heralding of the Good News, is the task of every Christian. Jesus said, "Go therefore and make disciples . . . teaching them to observe all that I have commanded" (Matt. 28:19– 20) and "Go out quickly into the streets and lanes of the city, and bring in hither the poor, and the maimed, and the halt, and the blind" (Luke 14:21).

While some would limit evangelism to specific areas such as personal soul winning, Scripture views the task as being much larger in scope. Every Christian is a witness in a very unique way and therefore is an evangelist in outreach for Christ. Jesus acknowledged the breadth of heralding the gospel when he read, "The spirit of the Lord is upon me, because he hath anointed me to preach the gospel to the poor; he hath sent me to heal the brokenhearted, to preach deliverance to the captives, and recovering of sight to the blind, to set at liberty them that are bruised" (Luke 4:18). Each age may demand new methods of evangelism, but the message of redemption remains the same.

Visitation is a part of our Christian ministry. In an age of computerized technology, condominiums, and word processors, we have difficulty finding time to visit very much with other persons. But James wrote, "Religion that is pure and undefiled before God and the Father is this: to visit orphans and widows in their affliction, and to keep oneself unstained from the world" (1:27). Even families have little time for person-to-person conversation and listening. The believer in Christ places greater value on persons than programs and profits. Jesus had time to visit with the woman at the well (John 4:1—30) and it changed her life and the community in which she lived. Visitation maintains communication among the family of God and serves as a contact with the world in which we live. Orphanages, nursing homes, prisons, hospitals, and retirement centers are only a few of the opportunities to minister through visitation.

Social ministries, or those services extended by the people of God to relieve human suffering, become the privilege of each believer. Jesus mentioned many of these responsibilities in Matthew 25:31—46, as he referred to our accountability in the Judgment. He spoke of the naked, the hungry, the thirsty, the imprisoned, the sick, all representing the needs of humanity to which we are to minister. This ministry has been hindered by those who divide the gospel into personal and social categories. There is only one gospel, and it mandates that true evangelism must consider the personal and social needs of every person. The displaced person who has been dehumanized by the cultural caste systems of our day needs to know that the Church cares. If we are the body of Christ, then we must demonstrate Jesus' compassion for those caught up in the disasters of human experience.

Preaching and teaching enable us to equip others to share in the opportunities that God gives to his Church. While questioned by some, a need will always exist for the proclamation of the gospel. Paul wrote, "It pleased God through the folly of what we preach to save those who believe" (1 Cor. 1:21). For that very reason God gives gifts to prepare us to serve adequately. Again Paul wrote, "And his gifts were that some should be apostles, some prophets, some evangelists, some pastors and teachers" (Eph. 4:11). With the continued increase in world population and new discoveries in communications, we are to share this message with all people. There is a need for preachers and teachers both locally and worldwide. Jesus said, "Lift up your eyes, and look on the fields; for they are white already to harvest" (John 4:35).

As servants of God there is a place of ministry for every believer. To follow the example of Christ we must be willing to meet needs wherever they are to be found. We are committed to serve wherever the Lord places us (1 Cor. 12:18).

Questions for Study, Chapter 12

1. According to Jesus' example, what is the first priority in preparing to minister to the needs of others? (See Mark 1:35 and Matthew 9:38.)

_____

2. What does the phrase "priesthood of all believers" mean to you? (See Revelation 1:6 and 1 Peter 2:9.)

_____

_____

_____

3. Paul lists for us at least eighteen different gifts of the Spirit (1 Cor. 12; Rom. 12; Eph. 4). Study these gifts and attempt to discover what gift or gifts God has given you. If you are not certain, discuss it with your pastor or church school teacher.

4. Why is it difficult in some congregations for spiritual gifts to be exercised? Discuss and reflect on the location of 1 Corinthians 13 in Paul's letter to the Corinthians — is love the determining factor?

_____

_____

5. According to Matthew 28:19–20, is evangelism the only task of the Church? If so, please define what you mean by evangelism. _____

_____

6. How many visits have you made in the last six months that were initiated by the need of others or the prompting of the Holy Spirit?_____ What, according to James 1:27, does this say about your personal relationship with God?

7. With our emphasis upon preaching and teaching in the church, how can we implement the teaching of social ministry as referred to in Matthew 25:31–46? _____

_____

_____

Memorize:

But whosoever will be great among you, let him be your minister; and whosoever will be chief among you, let him be your servant.
—Matthew 20:27–28

Chapter 13

The Kingdom of God: A Present Reality

Jesus came to establish a spiritual kingdom. When before Pilate, he said, "My kingship is not of this world; if my kingship were of this world, my servants would fight, that I might not be handed over the Jews" (John 18:36). Christ rejected the idea of an earthly, carnal kingdom. Every kingdom that has been built by force has fallen; and if Christ's kingdom were established on the same principle, it would be no better than the kingdoms of this world. An earthly kingdom is inadequate for God's kingdom.

The kingdom of God is not political, nor is it comprised only of Jewish people. Everything about the kingdom is spiritual. It is composed of spiritual people who have been born again. Paul wrote,

"For he is not a Jew, which is one outwardly; neither is that circumcision, which is outward in the flesh: But he is a Jew, which is one inwardly; and circumcision is that of the heart, in the spirit, and not in the letter, whose praise is not of men, but of God" (Rom. 2:28– 29). The Kingdom has a spiritual city as its central rallying point (the heavenly Jerusalem). Spiritual battles are fought. The Kingdom will last not just for one thousand years; "[God] shall reign over the house of Jacob forever; and of his kingdom there shall be no end" (Luke 1:33). This agrees with Daniel's prophecy of an everlasting kingdom. Christ established this kingdom at his first coming.

The kingdom of God is a spiritual experience. Jesus taught his disciples to "seek first [God's] kingdom" (Matt. 6:33). He declared, "The kingdom of God is preached, and every one enters it violently" (Luke 16:16). The kingdom of God is a spiritual inheritance. Paul wrote, "He has delivered us from the domination of darkness and transferred us to the kingdom of his beloved Son" (Col. 1:13). (Note that this act of God is already accomplished.) Entrance into the kingdom is by the experience of the new birth, for Jesus said, "Unless one is born anew, he cannot see the kingdom of God" (John 3:3). Consequently, to be born again is to be in the Kingdom.

Paul emphasizes the spiritual nature of the Kingdom by saying, "For the kingdom of God is not food and drink but righteousness and peace and joy in the Holy Spirit" (Rom. 14:17). He again records this testimony, "Flesh and blood cannot inherit the kingdom of God" (1 Cor.

15:50). This kingdom does not signify some future earthly reign; it represents the reign of righteousness enjoyed by the people of God since Christ came to proclaim it. Already the people of this kingdom were "kings and priests unto God" (1 Pet. 2:9). Paul declares that "they which receive abundance of grace and of the gift of righteousness shall reign in the life by one, Jesus Christ" (Rom. 5:17).

Christ is universal king, Lord of heaven and earth. Before his ascension he claimed this dominion saying, "All power is given unto me in heaven and in earth" (Matt. 28:18). This universal dominion is also expressed by Paul: "Which he wrought in Christ, when he raised him from the dead, and set him at his own right hand in the heavenly places, far above all principality, and power, and might, and dominion, and every name that is named, not only in this world, but also in that which is to come: and hath put all things under his feet, and gave him to be the head over all things" (Eph. 1:20–22).

Yes, Christ is king in the present tense. He has already conquered sin and death. His subjects acknowledge his sovereign lordship and wait expectantly for his return.

Questions for Study, Chapter 13

1. According to Mark 1:14, what did Jesus come into Galilee preaching?

2. Who are the subjects of Christ's kingdom and how do they gain acceptance? (See Matthew 18:3 and John 3:13.) _____

3. According to John 19:36, is the kingdom of God one of military might?

4. Great importance is placed upon the Jewish nation and its place in Kingdom teachings. In your own words, explain what Paul says in Romans 2:28–29 about the true Jew.

5. In what manner did Jesus speak of his kingdom in Luke 13:18–21)?

6. Paul clearly states the nature of the Kingdom in Romans 14:17. List what it is and what it is not _____

_____

_____

7. Kings are in control, having power to accomplish their purpose. According to Matthew 28:18, is Christ the King in control today?

_____

_____

Memorize:

> The Kingdom of God cometh not with observation: Neither shall they say, Lo here! or, lo there! for, behold, the kingdom of God is within you.
>
> —Luke 17:20– 21

Chapter 14

The End of Time: Jesus Comes Again

We are living between two advents of Christ in this world. At the first he appeared incarnate to reveal the way of salvation and to make atonement for sin. He will come again at some future time in great power and glory to raise the dead, judge the world, and destroy the earth.

That Christ will come again to the world is the common belief of Christians of all schools of thought. But those who believe the New Testament have abundant proof that Jesus will surely come again. "When I go and prepare a place for you, I will come again and will take you to myself" (John 14:3). "As the lightning comes from the east and shines as far as the west, so will be the coming of the Son of man" (Matt. 24:27).

"The Lord himself will descend from heaven" (1 Thess. 4:16). "Our commonwealth is in heaven, and from it we await a Savior, the Lord Jesus Christ" (Phil. 3:20). "Christ, having been offered once to bear the sins of many, will appear a second time, not to deal with sin but to save those who are eagerly waiting for him" (Heb. 9:28). The Scriptures clearly teach a second, personal, visible coming of Christ that is yet to come.

As the straining eyes of the wondering disciples saw their ascending Lord rise higher and higher until a cloud finally obscured him from their view, two angels said to them, "Men of Galilee, why do you stand looking into heaven? This Jesus, who was taken up from you into heaven, will come in the same way as you saw him go into heaven" (Acts 1:11). As Jesus' ascension was visible and personal, so will be his second advent, according to these words from Matthew: "Hereafter you will see the Son of man seated at the right hand of Power, and coming on the clouds of heaven" (26:64). The disciple also records these words of Jesus: "Then all the tribes of the earth will mourn, and they will see the Son of man coming on the clouds of heaven with power and great glory" (Matt. 24:30). The Book of Revelation declares, "Behold, he is coming with the clouds, and every eye will see him, everyone who pierced him; and all tribes of the earth will wail on account of him" (1:7).

The time when Christ will return to earth is fully known to God. That he does know it is affirmed by Paul: "He has fixed a day on which he will judge the world" (Acts 17:31).

But while God knows the time of the second coming of Christ, it is known to no person. Jesus said, "Of that day and hour no one knows, not even the angels of heaven, nor the Son, but the Father only" (Matt. 24:36). To most persons living when he comes, the advent of Christ will be unexpected. It is not to be preceded by any great change in the natural order of things. Jesus explained, "As were the days of Noah, so will be the coming of the Son of man. For as in those days before the flood they were eating and drinking, marrying and giving in marriage, until the day when Noah entered the ark, and they did not know until the flood came and swept them all away, so will be the coming of the Son of man" (Matt. 24:37–39). In this text the moral state of the world at Christ's coming is not under consideration. It merely shows that as that awful catastrophe came suddenly and without warning, so the second advent will be unexpected by the world at large. Peter wrote, "The day of the Lord will come like a thief" (2 Pet. 3:10).

A *general resurrection* is taught by the Bible, as is indicated in the following scriptures. "Many of them that sleep in the dust of the earth shall awake, some to everlasting life, and some to shame and everlasting contempt" (Dan. 12:2). "The hour is coming when all who are in the tombs will hear his voice and come forth, those who have done good, to the resurrection of life, and those who have done evil, to the resurrection of judgment" (John 5:28, 29). "There will be a resurrection of both the just and unjust" (Acts 24:15).

All these texts clearly teach a general resurrection. The same truth is definitely implied in the texts that state that the righteous shall be raised up "at the last day" (John 6:39,40,44,54). There is no day after the last day, and no resurrection can take place a thousand years after the last day. That the dead will be raised at the time of the second advent is clear from 1 Thessalonians 4:16 and 1 Corinthians 15:21 – 23.

The Scriptures very definitely set forth the fact of *a future judgment:* "The Lord knows how to rescue the godly from trial, and to keep the unrighteous under punishment until the day of judgment" (2 Pet. 2:9); "He has fixed a day on which he will judge the world in righteousness by a man whom he has appointed" (Acts 17:31); "We shall all stand before the judgment seat of God" (Rom. 14:10); "It shall be more tolerable on the day of judgment for the land of Sodom than for you" (Matt. 11:24). The people of Sodom had long since died, but Jesus here represents their judgment as yet to come. It will be coincident with the advent of Christ.

The most elaborate and specific account of the Judgment given in the Bible is that contained in Matthew 25:31 – 46, where it is represented as taking place immediately following the second coming of Christ. Jesus said, "The Son of man is to come with his angels in the glory of his Father, and then he will repay every man for what he has done" (Matt. 16:27). And Paul wrote, "Christ Jesus . . . is to judge the living and the dead" (2 Tim. 4:1).

The Judgment will take place after the general resurrection. Jesus declared, "For the hour is coming, when all who are in the tombs will hear his voice and come forth, those who have done good, to the resurrection of life, and those who have done evil, to the resurrection of judgment" (John 5:28,29). The distribution of reward and punishment subsequent to the resurrection implies judgment. John wrote, "And I saw the dead, great and small, standing before the throne, and books were opened. Also another book was opened, which is the book of life. And the dead were judged by what was written in the books, by what they had done. And the sea gave up the dead in it, Death and Hades gave up the dead in them, and all were judged by what they had done" (Rev. 20:12,13).

The statement that the sea gave up the dead who were in it implies the resurrection. Subsequent to that, the judgment is said to occur at the end of the world: " 'Let both grow together until the harvest; and at harvest time I will tell the reapers, Gather the weeds first and bind them in bundles to be burned, but gather the wheat into my barn.' . . . The harvest is the close of the age. . . . So will it be at the close of the age" (Matt. 13:30,39,40).

The future judgment will be a general judgment in the sense that all people both good and evil will be judged at one and the same time. The Scriptures are replete with such proofs. Several texts already quoted concerning the future judgment represent it as a general judgment. This is especially clear in the discourse of Jesus recorded in Matthew 25:31 – 46.

The Word of God is the primary standard of judgment. In the nature of things, people are obligated to obey whatever commandments God has given them. But they are responsible and subject to God's law only so far as that law has been given to them. Jesus said, "The word that I have spoken will be his judge on the last day" (John 12:48). Paul said, "All who have sinned without the law will also perish without the law, and all who have sinned under the law will be judged by the law" (Rom. 2:12).

Future Punishment: Hell

The doctrine of future punishment is supported by both scriptural and rational proofs.

The Scriptures represent the punishment of the wicked as taking placed after the close of this life: "The rich man also died and was buried; and in Hades, being in torment, he lift up his eyes," (Luke 16:22,23). The wicked will be punished when Christ comes again: "For the Son of man is to come with his angels in the glory of his Father, and then he will repay every man for what he has done" (Matt. 16:27). The future punishments of the wicked are represented as being by "eternal fire" (Matt. 25:41); they will be cast into a "lake that burns with fire and sulphur" (Rev. 21:8) or a "furnace of fire" (Matt. 13:42). The wicked are to be thrown into "outer darkness" (Matt. 8:12), or into "gloom of darkness" (Jude 13). They are to have "no rest, day or night" (Rev. 14:11), undergoing pain of a "second death" (Rev. 21:8) and "eternal destruction, away from the presence of the Lord" (2 Thess. 1:9, NAS).

102

Future Blessedness: Heaven

Future blessedness is to be experienced in heaven. This is a truth of both the Scriptures and reason. In the Scriptures it is represented as being "eternal life" (Matt. 25:46), "eternal weight of glory" (2 Cor. 4:17), knowledge (1 Cor. 13:8–10), worship (Rev. 19:1), association with holy men and angels (Heb. 12:22–23), and as communion with God (Rev. 21:3).

The happiness of the righteous in heaven will consist of various elements. (1) They will be secure from the possibility of being lost forever. (2) They will be forever free from all earthly sorrow and pain. John wrote, "[God] . . . will wipe away every tear from their eyes, and death shall be no more, neither shall there be mourning nor crying nor pain any more" (Rev. 21:4). They shall no longer be tempted by sin or troubled by sinful surroundings. (3) They will then know God as they are now known of him. "They shall see his face" (Rev. 22:4) and "see him as he is" (1 John 3:2). (4) The righteous will there have joyful fellowship with all the holy and truly great. (5) The righteous will have the opportunity for indefinite enlargement of all faculties. We may well believe that the righteous will live and learn forever there.

The reality that these wonderful facts represent is probably beyond the capacity of our finite minds. As Paul wrote, "No eye has seen, nor ear heard, nor the heart of man conceived what God has prepared for those who love him" (1 Cor. 2:9).[11]

Questions for Study, Chapter 14

1. Some self-styled prophets have attempted to predict the exact time of Christ's return. What does Scripture say about this? (See Matthew 24:27, 36.) _____

2. While some speak of an erroneous "secret rapture" when Jesus returns, how does this correlate with Revelation 1:7? _____

3. Will there be only *one* or *two* returns of Christ? Some present teachings imply that Jesus will return once to catch away his bride, the Church, and again to judge the world. Consider 1 Thessalonians 4:16—17 and 1 Corinthians 15:21—24.

_____

4. There will be only one general resurrection, leaving no room for a supposed millennial reign. Consider Acts 24:15 and John 6:39, 40, 44, 54. List your thoughts on this.____

_____

5. At the final judgment we will be judged by whom and by what standard? (See John 5:22; 12:48.)___

_____

6. Eternal retribution, or future punishment for sin, is clearly taught in Scripture. Using the following texts, indicate what you believe that punishment to be: Luke 16:22, 23; Matthew 25:41; Revelation 21:8. _____

_____

_____

7. Our human minds cannot conceive of what heaven — the reward of the righteous — will be like. From the description in Revelation 21:1 – 7, describe what you think it will be.

_____

_____

Memorize:

It is appointed unto men once to die, but after this the judgment.

— Hebrews 9:27

Notes:

1. Earl Martin, *Toward Understanding God* (Anderson, Ind.: Gospel Trumpet Company, 1942), p. 27.

2. F. G. Smith, *What the Bible Teaches*, condensed by Kenneth E. Jones (Anderson, Ind.: Warner Press, Inc., 1955), pp. 11–12.

3. H. Orton Wiley, *Christian Theology*, vol. 1 (Kansas City, Mo.: Beacon Hill Press, 1940), p. 168.

4. Russell R. Byrum, *Christian Theology*, 3rd ed. (Anderson, Ind.: Gospel Trumpet Co., 1950), pp. 323–324.

5. Charles E. Brown, *We Preach Christ* (Anderson, Ind.: Gospel Trumpet Co., 1957), p. 79.

6. Smith, *What the Bible Teaches*, p. 88.

7. Warren C. Roark, compiler, *The Holy Spirit* (Anderson, Ind.: Warner Press, 1947), pp. 75–80.

8. Byrum, *Christian Theology*, p. 556.

9. Smith, *What the Bible Teaches*, pp. 99–116.

10. Byrum, *Christian Theology*, pp. 493–498.

11. Ibid., pp. 634ff.